The Spanish Missions of Florida

ERIC SUBEN

Children's Press®
An Imprint of Scholastic Inc.
New York Toronto London Auckland Sydney
Mexico City New Delhi Hong Kong
Danbury, Connecticut

Content Consultant
Andrew K. Frank, Ph.D.
Department of History
Florida State University

Library of Congress Cataloging-in-Publication Data

Suben, Eric.
  The Spanish missions of Florida / by Eric Suben.
    p. cm.—(A true book)
  Includes bibliographical references and index.
  ISBN-13: 978-0-531-20578-5 (lib. bdg.)   978-0-531-21241-7 (pbk.)
  ISBN-10: 0-531-20578-9 (lib. bdg.)   0-531-21241-6 (pbk.)

1. Florida—History—Spanish colony, 1565-1763—Juvenile literature.
2. Missions, Spanish—Florida—History—Juvenile literature. 3.
Indians of North America—Missions—Florida—Juvenile literature. 4.
Franciscans—Missions—Florida—History—Juvenile literature. I. Title.
II. Series.

  F314.S893 2010
  975.9'01—dc22   2009018420

All rights reserved. Published in 2010 by Children's Press, an imprint of Scholastic Inc.
Published simultaneously in Canada. Printed in China.
SCHOLASTIC, CHILDREN'S PRESS, A TRUE BOOK, and associated logos are trademarks and/or registered trademarks of Scholastic Inc.

1 2 3 4 5 6 7 8 9 10 R 19 18 17 16 15 14 13 12 11 10   62

Find the Truth!

Everything you are about to read is true *except* for one of the sentences on this page.

Which one is **TRUE**?

T or F The first Spanish missions in what is now the United States were in Florida.

T or F Native Americans did not work at the Florida missions.

Find the answers in this book.

3

Contents

THE BIG TRUTH!

Mission Mystery

**A scientist studying
the ruins of a mission**

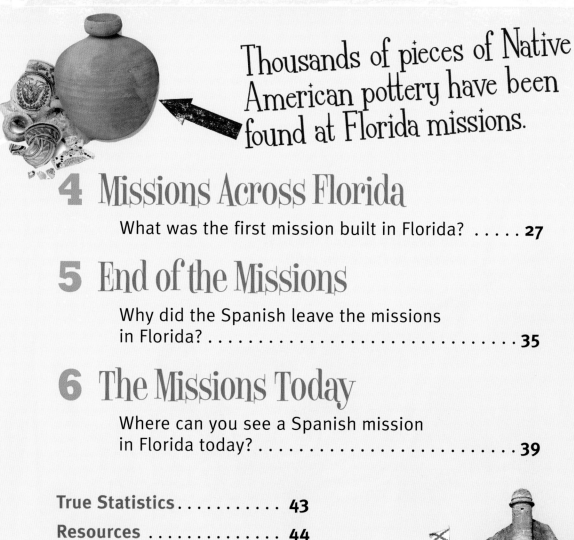

Thousands of pieces of Native American pottery have been found at Florida missions.

Castillo de San Marcos

The Spanish started the first mission in Florida in 1566.

CHAPTER 1

Europeans Arrive

In the late 1500s and the 1600s, Spain ruled over what is today the state of Florida. During this time, most of the people living in this area were Native Americans. The Spanish set up missions, or villages, close to where Native Americans had made their homes. At the missions, the Spanish forced Native Americans to work for them. They also tried to **convert** the Native people to Christianity and teach them Spanish ways of life.

Priests and soldiers traveled together to Florida to start missions.

Spain Takes Florida

In 1513, explorers from Spain first arrived in Florida. In 1565, King Philip II of Spain sent navy officer Pedro Menéndez de Avilés (PEH-dro meh-NEN-dez DEH ah-vee-LEHS) to Florida to start a **colony**. But Menéndez first had to battle the French, who were already in the area, for control of the region. Menéndez succeeded, and he began a Spanish **settlement** on Florida's east coast.

Menéndez sailed for Florida with 11 ships carrying about 2,000 people, including soldiers and sailors.

Menéndez (center) and his men build a village.

Building a Settlement

Menéndez called the settlement San Agustín (St. Augustine in English). In St. Augustine, the Spanish started a mission called Nombre de Dios (NOM-breh DEH DEE-os). They later built a

The Spanish began building Castillo de San Marcos in 1672.

stone fort called the Castillo de San Marcos (kas-TEE-yo DEH SAN MAR-kos) to help protect the settlement from raids by pirates and defend Spanish land from attacks by other nations.

Starting Missions

Missions were one way that Spain established its control over Florida. The Spanish built missions for many reasons. King Philip wanted to spread Christianity among Native Americans in Florida. He wanted them to give up their

A priest performs a special ceremony to welcome this baby into the Catholic church.

traditional ways of life, be **baptized** as Christians, and become more like the Spanish. The Spanish people in Florida also wanted Native people to work for them.

Priests and Friars

King Philip began sending priests called **missionaries** to Florida in 1566. The priests were ordered to start missions. As they set up the missions, the priests mistreated and angered the Native peoples. After a few years, the priests were not successful at converting the Native peoples, and they gave up and left Florida. King Philip then sent **friars** to start more Florida missions. Friars are religious men who preach and teach. The first friar arrived in 1573. In the years that followed, friars started missions throughout Florida.

A friar

More than 250,000 Timucuas lived in Florida when the Spanish arrived there.

CHAPTER 2

Learning to Live Together

When the Spanish arrived, Florida was home to hundreds of thousands of Native Americans. They lived in **chiefdoms**. Near St. Augustine, these chiefdoms included the Timucua (tih-MOO-kwuh) people and the Guale (WALL-ee) people, who lived farther north. To the west lived the Apalachee (ap-puh-LACH-ee) people.

Working for the Spanish

Many Spanish missions were started near existing Native American farms. The Spanish demanded a share of the crops grown at these farms. They also used Native people to do most of the work at the missions. Under a system called *repartimiento* (reh-par-tee-MYEN-toe), or "requirement," Native chiefs had to supply workers to the Spanish rulers. In exchange for the Natives' work, chiefs received guns, metal tools, glass beads, and other items that gave them more power and wealth. They shared some of these goods with the workers.

A group of Apalachee men put up a cross.

The Spanish sometimes protected Native people from attacks by other groups.

Helping Hands

Some Native leaders invited the Spanish to start missions among their people. These leaders felt the Spanish could protect them from attacks by other countries and their Native **allies**. Spanish soldiers also helped Native leaders who agreed to obey the Spanish king.

Timucua people prepare land for planting.

16

CHAPTER 3

Life at a Spanish Mission

The Spanish started dozens of missions among the Apalachee, Timucua, and Guale peoples, and other Native groups across northern and central Florida. They located these missions near large Native American villages because the villages could produce the extra crops that the Spanish wanted.

Some Native Americans accepted Christianity. Many of those who converted also continued to practice their traditional ways and beliefs.

← The Timucua grew corn, beans, squash, pumpkins, and melons.

The council house at Mission San Luis could hold more than 2,000 people.

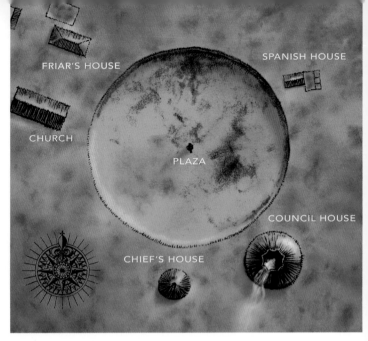

FRIAR'S HOUSE

SPANISH HOUSE

CHURCH

PLAZA

COUNCIL HOUSE

CHIEF'S HOUSE

This view from above shows how Mission San Luis (SAN loo-EES) was organized.

Mission Villages

Most Florida missions were organized in the same way. They had a church that faced an open area, or **plaza**. On the plaza, there was usually a council house where Native peoples held meetings. The friar's house, the houses of other Spanish people, and the chief's house were nearby. The homes of most Native peoples were located outside of this central area.

Mission Buildings

All mission buildings were constructed by Native American workers using both Spanish and Native building methods. They used Spanish construction materials such as iron nails. At the missions, the Native people built their own houses as they always had in their villages. They used wooden posts and made **thatched** roofs of dried leaves and grass.

The Timucua made the roofs of their houses from palm tree leaves.

In 1675, more than 1400 Native people lived at Mission San Luis and its surrounding villages.

Archaeologists are studying more than 1 million objects at Mission San Luis. Some are from the mission, and some are from other places.

Mission Mystery

Mission San Luis was destroyed in 1704. Eventually, the city of Tallahassee (ta-luh-HAH-see) was built on top of it. In 1983, archaeologists (ar-kee-AH-luh-jists) began digging where San Luis had been located. They discovered actual items from the mission. With these clues to San Luis's past, archaeologists were able to rebuild part of the mission and learn more about life there.

Each day, the plaza at Mission San Luis was filled with people, including soldiers, children, and merchants.

Hard Life

Native peoples worked hard at the Spanish missions. Besides constructing the buildings, Native people cooked, cleaned, and made all the goods that were needed. They also herded cattle and worked on farms. Under the Spanish *repartimiento* system, when Native men were ordered to work, they had to obey. Native people were often overworked, and they were sometimes beaten or mistreated by the Spanish.

Native peoples were forced to work for the Spanish.

By 1650, the Florida missions were growing 1 million pounds of corn each year.

Native people harvesting corn

Food and Farming

The Spanish introduced European crops to Florida's Native people. Some of the new crops included wheat, oranges, watermelons, peaches, and figs. With these new crops, Native women who cooked for the Spanish began blending Spanish and Native foods.

Pottery at the Missions

Native women made most of the pots used at the missions. Apalachee pots were found in both Spanish and Native people's homes at Mission San Luis. People used the pots for cooking and storing food. To make a pot, clay was rolled into long ropes. Then the ropes were wound into a spiral and smoothed. Sometimes the pots were decorated by pressing shells or corncobs against the clay.

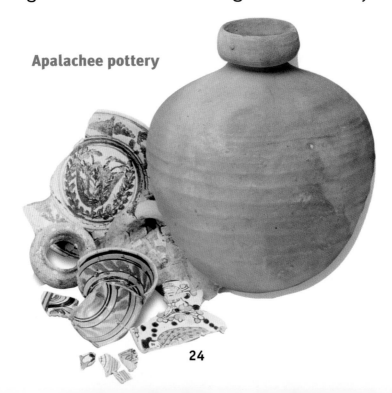

Apalachee pottery

A Game with Meaning

Life at the missions wasn't all work. In the spring and summer, the Apalachee people played a ball game that had religious meaning. They believed that the game pleased the spirits of thunder and rain, which would promise a good harvest. The object of the game was to kick a clay ball, wrapped in deerskin, into an empty eagle's nest that sat on top of a post. A team earned one point for hitting the post and two points for getting the ball into the nest. The team that first earned 11 points won the game.

People leave the church at Mission San Luis.

CHAPTER 4

Missions Across Florida

The Spanish built dozens of missions throughout Florida. The materials used to construct the missions included wood and palm trees found nearby. The construction materials were not very sturdy. No original mission buildings remain in Florida. Some burned down during attacks and **rebellions** by Native peoples. Other buildings slowly rotted away over the years.

Mission church bells were rung to let people know when it was time to pray, work, and eat.

Mission Nombre de Dios's church is so small that only 30 people can fit inside of it at one time.

Mission Nombre de Dios

The Spanish established Mission Nombre de Dios, in St. Augustine, soon after Pedro Menéndez de Avilés arrived in Florida. It was the first mission in today's United States. Nothing remains of the original mission, but a newer church stands on the site. Today, archaeologists are digging around the grounds at Mission Nombre de Dios to try to learn more about both Native and Spanish life in Florida.

Mission San Luis

Mission San Luis, in what is now Tallahassee, was one of the largest missions in Florida. The site where it was built was already an important Apalachee village when the Spanish built this mission. In 1656, the Spanish made San Luis their western capital in Florida. In the early 1700s, the British began attacking the Spanish in Florida. The Spanish and the Apalachee did not want the British to take over the mission. So in 1704 they burned and abandoned it.

It took 100,000 palm leaves to thatch the roof of Mission San Luis's rebuilt council house.

Mission San Francisco de Potano

Founded in 1606, Mission San Francisco de Potano (poh-TAH-no) stood near what is now the city of Gainesville, Florida. The mission included a church, a house for the friar, and a school. In 1656, the Timucua people who lived there rose up against the Spanish. This caused the Spanish to flee to St. Augustine. The Spanish returned a few years later.

Timucua people stuck arrows in the ground to declare war.

Talk the Talk

Being able to communicate with Native peoples at the missions was an important part of a friar's job. Father Francisco Pareja (pah-REH-hah) learned the language of the Timucua people and developed the first written form of it. He also translated religious books into the Timucua language. Because of Pareja's work, Timucua leaders were able to write to one another during a rebellion that lasted for eight months in 1656. This helped the Timucua communicate more easily over long distances.

31

British troops march south from Georgia to attack the Spanish in Florida.

Mission San Juan del Puerto

San Juan del Puerto (SAN WAN DEL PWER-toh) was one of Florida's longest-lasting missions. The Spanish started the mission in 1587 in what is now the city of Jacksonville. At the time, the Timucua people lived in this area. By 1602, about 500 Native people had converted to Christianity and lived at San Juan del Puerto. The mission was destroyed by British troops in 1702.

Mission Santa Fé de Toloca

Santa Fé de Toloca (toe-LOE-kah) stood near the Santa Fe River in northern Florida. Native Americans at the mission grew corn, wheat, and fruit that they carried in baskets to St. Augustine, a distance of about 80 miles (130 kilometers). Some of the crops and cattle they raised were sent by boat to the nearby island of Cuba. British soldiers burned the mission in 1702.

Ships carried crops from St. Augustine to other Spanish colonies.

Apalachees leave
Mission San Luis
as it burns.

CHAPTER 5

End of the Missions

By the early 1700s, Florida's missions were struggling to survive. Native American and British attacks destroyed some missions. At the same time, diseases from Europe had killed thousands of Native Americans. Because fewer Native people lived at Florida's missions, many of them were forced to close their doors. All of this caused the Spanish to abandon most of their missions in Florida.

The Spanish missions in Florida lasted almost 150 years.

Attacks on the Missions

Native Americans attacked and destroyed some missions in Florida because they were angry at how the Spanish had treated them. Then, in the 1700s, the British began invading Florida, trying to force the Spanish out of the area. They also destroyed some Spanish missions. At this time, some missions joined together or moved closer to cities such as St. Augustine for protection.

Florida Missions Timeline

1565
Pedro Menéndez de Avilés settles St. Augustine.

1566
King Philip II of Spain begins sending missionaries to Florida.

36

Disease Spreads

The Spanish brought new diseases such as measles and smallpox with them from Europe. The Native people of Florida had never before been exposed to these diseases. Their bodies could not fight them off. The diseases spread quickly through the missions, and thousands of people died.

As more Native people died from diseases, there were not enough of them left to do the work at the missions. This caused the Spanish to abandon many of Florida's missions.

1573
Friars arrive in Florida to start missions.

Early 1700s
Most of Florida's missions are destroyed or abandoned.

Memorial chapel on the site of Mission Nombre de Dios in St. Augustine

CHAPTER 6

The Missions Today

After the Spanish abandoned the missions, the buildings slowly fell into ruin. In the years that followed, people had forgotten where some of the missions had actually been located. At some former mission sites, such as Mission Nombre de Dios in St. Augustine, new churches have been built. People can now go to these churches to worship.

This church on the grounds of what was Mission Nombre de Dios was designed to look like a Spanish building from mission times.

Archaeologists working at Mission San Luis

Clues to the Past

In parts of Florida, archaeologists continue to search for the buried remains of mission buildings. They find the buildings by looking for nails, which were all that was left once the wood rotted away. They also look for items left behind by the people who lived at the missions. By studying items such as bones, pottery, and jewelry, archaeologists are able to understand more about how people lived at missions throughout Florida.

Visiting the Past

At Mission San Luis in the city of Tallahassee, visitors can experience what it was like to live at a Florida mission. From what archaeologists learned by studying this mission, people were able to rebuild San Luis's church, council house, and houses. Thousands of people visit the mission each year. Through these visits, they learn more about how Native and Spanish people lived in Florida long ago.

Visitors learn about a rebuilt Spanish house at Mission San Luis.

Lasting Effects

The Spanish missions in Florida lasted less than 150 years. During that time, they forever changed the lives of the Native peoples in the area. Diseases brought by the Spanish killed thousands of Native Americans. By the mid-1700s, most of the Native Americans in the region had died.

St. Augustine in the 1700s

Other changes brought by the Spanish extended beyond Florida. The horses, cattle, and crops that the Spanish brought to Florida were new to North America. Today, they continue to be a part of life in the United States. ★

The Spanish controlled St. Augustine until 1763.

True Statistics

First Spanish mission in what is now the United States: Mission Nombre de Dios

Number of Native people living under Spanish rule in Florida in the early 1500s: 350,000

Number of Native people living at the Florida missions at their peak: 26,000

Plants and animals the Spanish introduced to Florida: Peaches, oranges, wheat, figs, watermelons, cattle, horses

Did you find the truth?

T The first Spanish missions in what is now the United States were in Florida.

F Native Americans did not work at the Florida missions.

Resources

Books

Bial, Raymond. *Missions and Presidios.* New York: Children's Press, 2004.

Bredeson, Carmen. *Florida.* New York: Children's Press, 2002.

Brown, Robin C. *The Crafts of Florida's First People.* Sarasota, FL: Pineapple Press, 2003.

Crewe, Sabrina, and Janet Riehecky. *The Settling of St. Augustine.* Milwaukee, WI: Gareth Stevens, 2003.

Ditchfield, Christin. *Spanish Missions.* New York: Children's Press, 2006.

Knotts, Bob. *Florida History.* Chicago: Heinemann Library, 2008.

Thompson, William. *The Spanish Exploration of Florida.* Philadelphia: Mason Crest, 2003.

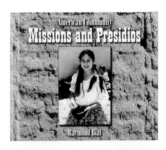

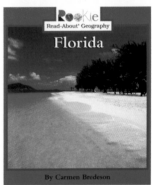

Organizations and Web Sites

Missions in Northeast Florida

www.nps.gov/timu/historyculture/missions_fgi.htm
Find out more about what mission life was like for Native Americans in northern Florida.

St. Augustine: America's Ancient City

www.flmnh.ufl.edu/staugustine/intro.htm
Take a virtual tour through the old city of St. Augustine.

Viva Florida: Spanish Missions

www.vivaflorida.org/Spanish+Missions.31.lasso
Explore Florida's mission history, and quiz yourself on the Kids Fun Page.

Places to Visit

Mission Nombre de Dios

27 Ocean Avenue
St. Augustine, FL 32084
(800) 342-6529
www.missionandshrine.org
Visit the site of the first Spanish mission in what is now the United States.

Mission San Luis

2100 West Tennessee Street
Tallahassee, FL 32304
(850) 487-3655
www.missionsanluis.org
Tour the rebuilt San Luis, one of the largest missions in Florida.

Important Words

allies – people working together for a common purpose

archaeologists (ar-kee-AH-luh-jists) – scientists who study what is left behind by people of the past

baptized – became a member of a church in a ceremony in which the person is sprinkled with or dipped in water

chiefdoms – societies in which many different villages are under the control of a chief

colony – a place where a group of people live together under the control of their home country

convert – to cause to accept different beliefs or ideas

friars – religious men who teach and preach. Not all friars are priests.

merchants – people who buy and sell goods

missionaries – people who try to convert others to their religion

plaza – a large open space in the center of a Spanish town

rebellions – fights against a government or others with power, usually by people seeking better treatment

settlement – a small village or place where people have recently chosen to live

thatched – covered with straw or other dried plants

Index

About the Author

Eric Suben is the author of more than 40 children's books and the coauthor of three guidebooks for writing children's books. Presently a lawyer, he was formerly the editor in chief of a leading children's book publishing company. He has taught children's book writing at several universities and writers' conferences. As a child, Suben lived for a time in South Florida, and he has a strong interest in American history, particularly the early voyages of exploration and European settlement of what is now the United States. Today, he lives in New York City with his wife and three children, who are avid readers of nonfiction.